1001 Decorating Ideas
Kitchens

Galahad Books • New York City

Contents

Introduction

Now that all appliances come in decorator colors and styles and pretty wallpapers are washable, designing a kitchen is a lot more fun. Depending on your needs, the kitchen can be set up as a work area for one or as a family gathering place. You might want a central work island for space-saving efficiency. Or, if the room is large enough, you might want to divide it into separate cooking, eating, and utility and storage areas. Kitchens in old houses or very small spaces present a special decorating challenge.
On the following pages are lots of ideas for turning your kitchen into an environment that is personal as well as functional—whether it be a room full of old-fashioned charm or a sleek, ultra-modern setting.

Many thanks to 1001 Decorating Ideas.

Chapter 1
Kitchens With Center Islands

Island work areas are the answer to many common kitchen problems. If you are short of wall space, it's a big help to place some of the major appliances in the center of the room. And if you need additional counters and cabinets, a work island supplies those as well. Add a couple bar stools, and an island can provide a convenient place to have a snack or coffee break, or to chat with the chef.

A cart is used here to create a portable center island that stores applicances and holds a cutting board and knives. Copper pots hang from a rack above the cart to complete the center island look. The counter-high cart can conveniently be stashed away in a corner or can roll up to any stationary counter to double its work space. Two different tile patterns are used in this kitchen: one on the floor, the other on the counter backs and cart. The tiles are coated with urethane for extra-high gloss and easy maintenance.

Photos: Alan Hicks/Design: GE & Neil Kelly Co.

This L-shaped kitchen has a multipurpose island that permits traffic to flow freely in all directions. Inlaid with ceramic tile, the island—which houses a cooktop—safely holds hot plates and pots. What's more, it is a convenient breakfast/snack bar as well as a serving counter for the adjacent family room. The kitchen appliances—a refrigerator/freezer, dishwasher and compactor in almond hue, plus a built-in wall oven and microwave—are placed for maximum efficiency and accessibility. Walnut-stained birch cabinets hold small appliances. Plants thrive in the window above the sink, while underfoot, the vinyl flooring shines without waxing. The range hood is painted in a rich red oxide color. The portable cart trundles china and flatware to the table in the adjacent dining area and, after meals, carries them to the dishwasher.

If you love the look of brick but can't afford to pay for extensive foundation work and highly skilled labor, don't despair. In this "brick"-walled kitchen with a decidedly country air, do-it-yourself brick look-alikes are used. The center island, with the built-in range, doubles as a chopping block and counter for eating at all

continued

hours. The versatile range is outfitted with a re-movable, open-spit rotisserie grill and a ceramic cooktop. It operates as a conventional oven or as a convected power oven for faster roasting, and is continuously self-cleaning.

The built-ins include hand-crafted cabinets with a wood finish, a microwave oven, and a wine rack. A dishwasher solves the who-does-the-dishes problem, and the refrigerator features an automatic ice-maker. Above the sink is a greenhouse window, which adds a welcome cool contrast to the warm, red "brick." The plants sit in a special trough filled with gravel for drain-age and plant humidification. Underfoot, the floor-ing is cushioned vinyl in a subtle parchment color. The sign "Mom's Bakery" is painted with brilliant acrylics above the cedar strip with dowels for holding pots and pans.

Here is a view of the greenhouse window above the sink. The greenery provides the only color contrast to the red-browns of the wood and bricks. It also provides enough privacy so that no curtains are necessary to cover the window.

Photos: Jack Evans/Design: Paul Bergen

The loaves of bread are being painted with acrylic paint above the "Mom's Bakery" sign here. Below the sign is the cedar strip that is handy for holding utensils and pots.

This kitchen-breakfast nook has weathered white paneling, almond appliances, and an off-white counter top. The center island divides the eating area from the kitchen work area and supplies additional counter space. The side facing the table is covered in print paper that matches the wall covering in the room and hallway, and the living room curtains. Sunlight pours through a large skylight and a greenhouse window. A no-wax floor in a brick pattern establishes a polished yet rustic ambience, bolstered by the rich copper tones of the molds and kettles.

Photos: Yuichi Idaka/Design: Richard Honquest & J. Christopher Jones

Built-in fluorescent lighting illuminates this kitchen four ways: For general lighting, it edges the entire perimeter at ceiling level; for task lighting, it is installed around the perimeter of the custom hood, under the cabinets, and above the sink. The center island is extra practical here. It has counter space for chopping and serving food, a range, cabinet space underneath for additional storage, and a shelf and display area up top to keep favorite bowls and utensils close at hand. The hood is designed with wood strips that can be used to hold hanging pots or to support a plate collection.

Here's a great setup for a quick snack, conveniently located in the center of the kitchen cooking area. In addition to providing eating space, the center island supplies additional counter space. With the hanging pot rack over the island, the center of the kitchen becomes the room's focal point. Three-tiered wire baskets and a long spice rack help keep counter space uncluttered. The carpet, a beige and tan hopsacking of nylon filament, is so tightly woven that it won't absorb that inevitable, occasional spill. The multicolored pattern also helps hide soiling.

Design: Virginia Wood

Photo: Everette Short/Design: Evan Frances, ASID, & J. Christopher Jones

unlight pours through white blinds in this kitchen's window, illuminating the terra cotta-colored counter top with a round-edged seamless work surface that makes cleanup a breeze. Cabinets in deep pecan wood with cinnamon finish are the perfect foil for the other decorating elements in the room: clay-colored floor tile and wall paint in a soft flesh tone. Bar stools slip under an island lighted by a skylight during daylight hours, by four track-mounted cylinders after dark. Miniaturized track lighting is under the cabinets.

In this renovated barn's kitchen, an island cooktop in natural wood is the culinary heart of the house. The wood beams, rafters, and ceramic quarry-tile floor play against a lively checked vinyl wall covering. High swiveling bar stools serve as seating at the counter, which has a beautiful view of sugar maples and apple trees. The island cooktop has a built-in grill.

Photo: Darwin Davidson/Design: Barbara K. Thorsen

Chapter 2
Kitchens With Breakfast Nooks

There's nothing more convenient than having a place to eat in or close to the kitchen, so that dishes and food don't have to be carried a great distance. Some kitchens just happen to have a corner or alcove that's perfect for a small table and chairs. Others are designed so that they flow into an adjacent dining room. With some remodeling and a little imagination, a breakfast nook can be created in any kitchen.

This spacious, many-windowed kitchen was planned to provide space in which a large family could congregate and cook together. It features oak cabinets, stain-resistant counter tops, and asbestos nox-wax flooring. One-inch blinds control light and reveal a lovely view. Affordable curtains are fashioned from sheets (one king-sized sheet per panel) and hang from a decorative traverse rod. When it's not mealtime, the handsome chandelier over the table makes a great study-homework lamp. The 42-inch-diameter fiberglass table has a pedestal base so no one has to straddle the table legs awkwardly. The tabletop, which resists spills and stains, is perfect for a houseful of children.

Here are two more views of the kitchen on page 20. Above is a closeup of the table, with its pedestal base and stain-resistant top. The cheery yellow and red table setting picks up the color accents used throughout the kitchen. To the right is a view of the large room. Plants are placed on top of all the cabinets to add color and texture. A chair matching the dining set pulls up to a small telephone counter.

Darwin Davidson/Design: Stylecraft

23

In a corner of this kitchen, under the windows, a small alcove is used for a round table and chairs. Lots of plants, floral wallpaper, and the sunny white and yellow colors give this area a garden-room look. Tiny plants in braid-trimmed strawberry boxes sit on glass shelves. The white "slicker" tablecloth is trimmed with decorative braid at its hemline. Yellow and white polka-dot fabric is fashioned into runners with end tassels, into removable and washable seat pads, and into shirred shades for the chandelier lights. Vinyl wall covering frames the area. The dark brick vinyl asbestos flooring is a dramatic foil for the white walls, tablecloth, and chairs.

Design: Nance Randol

From this kitchen, the cook can be included in the goings on in the adjacent family room. Major appliances are in a deep coffee color, which goes well with the kitchen cabinets and the blue and brown plaid vinyl flooring, selected for its resiliency, easy cleaning, and no-wax properties. The highly durable counter top is a bright blue, chosen because it recalls the blue of the fabric on the walls of the family room. The breakfast area has a box window that boasts vertical louvers in a floral pattern, which coordinates with the area's wallpaper. An adroit lighting arrangement employs two parallel tracks, with flexible light sources that house bulbs of high or low wattage for the different kinds of kitchen tasks.

Vinyl wall covering is run horizontally in the dinette area of this kitchen. It coordinates with vinyl flooring in an orange and white plaid. Wallpaper that matches the dining room drapery is used as a border over the kitchen cabinets. The round wood table in the kitchen can be used for breakfast and snacks. The more formal dining area is just as conveniently located off the kitchen. The "window" between the rooms provides a serving ledge and stops the cook from feeling cut off from dining room activities.

This kitchen is done completely in black and white. Cabinet doors are framed with black routing. The wall between the cabinets and the counter tops matches the black Formica of the counters. The total effect is starkly contemporary and clean. Alternate black and white vinyl flooring squares and a white pedestal table help complete the black and white look. China, napkin rings, linens, and even the cat's bowl are in the two-color scheme of this pristinely modern kitchen.

choolhouse chairs, a wood peg coatrack, and wood wall sconces create a country flavor in this dining nook and adjacent kitchen. The eating and cooking areas are unified by the wallpaper and the no-wax vinyl flooring. The countrified kitchen is modernized by an island "slave" that follows from one chore to another; it's a custom-made cube that moves easily on casters to put extra work surface and storage within easy reach anywhere in the kitchen. A window greenhouse makes a healthy home for greenery above the sink and repeats the openness of the bay window in the breakfast nook. The brass accessories reflect light, adding spark to the navy, white, and wood color scheme. In the dining area, a wallpaper-covered table repeats the mini-print pattern of the walls, and a plushly pillowed window seat expands seating potential.

Photos: Bill Hedrich/Design: Patricia Laughman & J. Christopher Jones

Photos: Everette Short/Design: Ellyn Carol Hirsch

◄ Succulent pears, apples, and grapes border the stained-glass, Tiffany-style shade in the breakfast area of this kitchen. The two areas are divided by a counter, which also is useful as a serving surface for the dining table. In the cooking area, cane-weave panels and brass hardware adorn the smoothly sculpted oak cabinets; a built-in wine rack over the spice rack stashes a gourmet's cache of reds and whites. Mounted above the cooktop is a microwave oven, conveniently placed at eye level. Above the cabinets, hanging copper pots are used as planters, which tie into the greenery motif of the wallpaper and the plants in front of all the windows.

Here, a family relaxes in their kitchen. Since the room gets almost no direct natural light, a bright canary yellow and white geometric wall covering is used everywhere to simulate sunshine. Austrian shades, in a washable cotton print to match the walls, can be pulled all the way up to bare the large window and to admit every drop of available light. The deep shelf at window-sill height is used both as a spot to grow plants and as a server. Family meals are often eaten around the butcher block kitchen table, which doubles as a work surface when large meals are being prepared.

Photo: Richard Champion/Design: Carleton Varney

O n bright days, the sun streams in through the skylight and windows of this kitchen, the Chinese red takes on a more orange hue, and the whole kitchen is filled with color. But on gray days, the peach color accents feel warm and the Chinese red seems even redder and more cheerful. Both the skylight and windows are part of a five-foot addition onto the kitchen, which was built in order to expand the breakfast nook. The old kitchen cabinets were stripped and repainted peach and red to go with the tricolor blinds covering the windows and door. Everything in the room is washable: The blinds, the cabinets, and the floor all can be easily cleaned.

Photo: Ray Grisbol/Design: Ken Stanley & Judy Spence for Neil Kelly Co.

This dining alcove off the kitchen has built-in banquettes that seat six. The small area has been kept visually spacious by the use of a bright, clean color scheme of white and kelly green. The print cushions bring color and pattern to the alcove without "weighing" it down. Green Belgian linen and polyester napkins, smaller than place mats, conserve space and make the table seem larger. The rear wall of mirror squares seems to double the space of the room.

Photo: Everette Short/Design: Lois Munroe Hoyt, ASID

Photos: Vince Lisanti/Design: Nance Randol & Joanne Kinn

This kitchen and adjoining breakfast nook are designed for good looks, convenience, and sociability. The kitchen's ultra-efficient work island is within sight and sound of the family room; the cook can chat with family members and guests rather than work in isolation. The outside of the island, which is seen both from the breakfast nook and from the family room, is faced with wall covering that coordinates with the fabric used in the family room and on the nook's sliding glass doors leading to the patio. Vinyl flooring and yellow and white checked wallpaper link the kitchen and dining areas. Base cabinets in the kitchen are painted yellow to match the wall covering. In the breakfast nook, the table and chairs and the chandelier restate the Colonial theme of the family room beyond.

◄ The outdoors is carried into this breakfast nook through glass patio doors covered in color-coordinated wood shades and curtains. The wrought-iron chairs pick up the subtle scroll effect in the pattern that appears on the wall and the chair seats. A floor-length tablecloth in solid brown echoes the darkest coloration in the curtains and the deepest shade in the ceramic tile floor. On the wall, an antique English spoon rack adds yet another textural note.

Photo: Everette Short/Design: Jan Rankin

This gallery kitchen and dining alcove are unified by the vinyl resilient flooring and are visually expanded by pale tones of green in the stone and mortar pattern used throughout. Self-adhesive wall tiles define the separate yet well-integrated areas.

Photos: Everette Short/Design: Evan Frances, ASID, & J. Christopher Jones

Wood furniture, cabinets, and paneling give a rustic look to this kitchen/dining room. The clay-colored floor tiles and soft flesh wall paint blend smoothly with the rich wood tones. Cabinets divide the eating from the cooking area and provide a serving counter for the dining area. A touch of greenery brightens the brown color scheme and links the room to the patio outdoors, which is surrounded by greenery.

A new kitchen was built in this house, and what was once the old kitchen was turned into an adjoining dining area. The two areas are linked by cream colored walls, wood trim, wood cabinets and furniture, and hanging plants in front of all the windows. Plastic stacking storage bins—in the same gold shade as the refrigerator, other small appliances, and flower pots—are placed next to the refrigerator. The gold is picked up in the dining room, with the gold glasses and flowered plates.

Photos: Alan Hicks

38

ots of oak-finished storage cabinets, in every conceivable dimension for every conceivable purpose, are the main feature of this L-shaped kitchen/dining area. The cabinets opposite the butcher block-topped table are only 12 inches deep; they don't obstruct traffic, but they do hold china and provide a surface for informal serving. Above that surface is a built-in toaster to keep counter space clear. The kitchen work area has a built-in can opener, paper towel dispenser, and shallow built-in pantry camouflaged by the wall covering.

Color unifies the kitchen and eating area. The wallpaper continues around the bend; so does the ceramic tile on the floor and beneath the cabinets. Ceramic tile is as functional as it is fashionable—the inevitable spills and spatters are easily wiped up. The yellow counter tops support sleek orange bowls, utensils, and foodsavers. The bright orange and yellow color scheme is continued in the drapery fabric, which is tied back over vertical blinds covering the patio doors. And behind the table is a handwoven wall hanging that picks up the room's colors.

Photos: Vince Lisanti/Design: Michael Cannarozzi

The walls between three gloomy, small rooms were knocked out to create this open kitchen. A work island was placed in the middle of the room to provide a serving surface close to the dining area and a roomy storage cabinet to hold all entertaining needs. It also disguises the load-bearing posts that could not be removed when the walls were knocked down. Child-proof materials were selected when the kitchen was redecorated, including no-wax vinyl flooring and a carefree, marble-like material for the sink and all counter tops. Installing a lowered ceiling of noise-depressant material unified the diverse ceilings encountered when the walls were removed. Swiveling track and spot lighting illuminates the kitchen.

The cabinets were built to store everything, including the garbage can. Their interiors are organized for total space utilization. The kitchen design also incorporates a special "safety" knife drawer, a vertically divided cabinet next to the stove for baking tins, and pull-out shelves to hold heavy cooking gear. Four-inch-deep shelves, fitted into a narrow space along one wall, hold cans.

The modern dining area is placed by the old kitchen windows. Toys and games are thoughtfully stashed in cabinets near the table, encouraging family fun in this delightful spot. A grill hides the radiator, and there's a wood drop-leaf shelf next to the table.

Photos: John Blanding

This charming dining nook is bursting with pattern. There's pattern on the walls, at the window, on the table cover and chair seats, and even on the floor. The wide-board floor is painted red with deck enamel and spattered with white—a rustic effect that is as practical as it is pretty, since the spatter pattern conceals dirt and foot marks. The decorative motifs glued on the chair tops, front and back, are cut from the wall covering. And the hanging metal shade is a tractor funnel bought at the hardware store; the designs are hammered in with an awl. A shelf installed in the window recess does double duty as desk and buffet. A teacart tucked neatly in the corner of the dining area makes the most of the limited space.

Chapter 3
Decorating With Wood

If not designed carefully, kitchens can be cold and antiseptic looking. Wood—used for cabinets, paneling, ceiling beams, or other furnishings—will give your kitchen a warm tone. It also will give the room an old-fashioned, rustic appearance that is a good foil for sleek, modern appliances. In a kitchen that's furnished or finished with wood, the wood tones exert an important effect on—in fact, they dominate—the overall color scheme.

This zigzag kitchen was originally a long, dark, tunnel-like space, with a view from the window of a bleak brick wall. The zigzags that shape the remodeled room are not merely a designer's fancy. In fact, the zigzags (each is precisely 45°) are necessary to make the kitchen really work. In a tight space, they permit easy access to the cooking area and ease the traffic flow back and forth to the breakfast room. The wall to an unused maid's room was ripped out to create ample space for the eating area. Everywhere else, a variety of resurfacing techniques camouflage the old kitchen. The buckling, water-stained ceiling disappeared behind a new dropped ceiling. The scarred walls vanished behind warm wood paneling. Above the sink, a tangle of pipes was masked and a handsome architectural look introduced with a built-in beam and light box. The dismal view of the brick wall is disguised by a woven window shade that also conceals the air conditioner.

continued on next page

In the cheery new dining area, the round table is illuminated by a light globe that is correctly hung just above eye level seated, or about 26 inches from the tabletop. The shelf and cabinet just below it store stoneware, a soup tureen, and an automatic coffee pot—all within easy reach of the table where they'll be used. The cabinet also holds table linens, glassware, and flatware.

In the kitchen area, a built-in cooktop with high speed, plug-in surface units, a self-cleaning oven, dishwasher, and sink are grouped in step-saving proximity. The paneled walls are a warm backdrop for a tool rack, botanical posters, and a wine rack. The refrigerator/freezer with textured steel doors has a work surface beside it, as does the cooktop and the durable enamel-on-cast-iron sink. Storage space for pots and pans is built-in directly above the wall oven. Underfoot, the pattern of the easy-care vinyl asbestos flooring echoes the roundness of the table and softens the vertical lines of the paneling and the angular built-in cabinets.

Photos: Ernest Silva/Design: Virginia Frankel

hen youngsters come dashing
through the door, they are usually
scurrying to their next activity. Providing a pegged "Raggedy Ann and
dy" tidy-up in this country casual mud room
ps them deposit outdoor gear in a neat and
eedy way.

Kitchens with wood flooring and furnishings
have a Colonial flavor. Here are two rooms that
seem to be transported from the 18th century.
Both have cupboards filled with pewter plates
and mugs, enhancing the old-fashioned effect.

Photos: Vince Lisanti/Design: Gaye & Rick Lopez

Knotty pine cabinets, beams, and hood give this kitchen a country feeling. Handsome Mexican tile covers the kitchen counters and behind the stove. White appliances and walls stop the wood effect from becoming too heavy. Antique baskets line the shelves and add texture, which is also provided by the rug in the dining area, the chair seats, and window shutters. A butcher block table is used as a small center work island. Plants in front of all the windows add a green accent color and add to the natural look of the room.

Photo: Robert Lautman

This kitchen, bedecked with dried herbs and flowers, exudes a deceptively old-fashioned air. Yet, apart from the lovingly preserved rolled-tin ceiling, it was designed, remodeled, and furnished from scratch. To achieve a natural look, ceramic tile is used for the floor and counter tops. The handsome kitchen cabinets, new table and chairs, and antique sideboard are solid oak. Bunches of dried brome grass, parsley, coriander, dill, and statice hang near the ceiling. The U-shaped work area is efficient and keeps the cook from feeling too isolated. Black glass doors cover the double oven. In front of the oven is an oval sisal rug, which absorbs the sound of footsteps on the ceramic tile floor. In the dining area, doilies are a lacy foil for the handsome stoneware coffee service on the sideboard. The antique sideboard and the table and chairs match the oak kitchen cabinets. There's an extra-long cord on the telephone so that it can reach the dining table.

Photos: Kent Oppenheimer

The graceful arches and stucco lace look of
Spanish Mission architecture inspired the design
of this remodeled kitchen. After the old kitchen
was gutted, wood beams were placed on the
ceiling, and the window wall was extended to
gain 100 square feet. An arched picture window
replaced the old, square window. To create a
barbecue area, a wall was torn down and the
arch motif repeated over the installed cooktop.
Wood cabinets and hanging greenery add a natural look.

In this wood-filled kitchen, the warm wood tones of the oak cabinetry and the ceiling beam, turned wood chandelier, and walnut-toned plastic laminate table are companionably linked with a wall of easy-to-install decorative "brick." The blue and green accents in the window shades, tiles, and plants both indoors and out the window add color accents. The center work island has a range, cutting board, drawers to hold utensils, and a rack to hold towels. Shelves along the kitchen's side wall hold storage jars and help keep counters clear.

This kitchen was remodeled to be more spacious and attractive. The old ceiling was raised and a beamed, wood-paneled cathedral ceiling—which visually expands the space and adds drama—was formed. A cobblestone-patterned vinyl floor and large-scale design wall covering unify the kitchen and dining areas. Shirred valances and café curtains, new walnut cabinets, a tile counter top, and chandeliers add a rustic warmth to this comfortable kitchen.

Photos: Kent Oppenheimer

Chapter 4
Kitchens in Old Houses

A kitchen in an old house often has unique decorating problems.
Its shape and size are not always the best possible for an efficient layout.
It may have pipes and radiators in strange places, and old appliances that
have to be worked around. It may have old plaster walls that are cracking,
and stained floors. But there are many ways—from major remodeling to
simple repainting—of creating a new kitchen, while still keeping the charm of
an old one.

It's the combination of floor and wall tiles that makes the mood Mediterranean in this remodeled kitchen. Extra-high cabinets, a second window, an air conditioner, and a washer and dryer are all expertly camouflaged, closed off, or otherwise concealed by the wall covering and cabinets. The careful attention to camouflage serves to highlight the Mediterranean mood, which is enhanced by adobe-colored vinyl flooring played against walnut-stained cabinets. Wall covering conceals the extra-high cabinets that are hung almost entirely around the kitchen, their sliding doors just barely detectable by the matching border (applied upside down on purpose for a better blend with the ceiling). A skinny window, a holdover from the old kitchen, is hidden behind a cabinet door and is used to vent the range hood and the washer and dryer. The window air conditioner is craftily concealed too. Installed in a transom above the remaining window, it's screened by shutters faced with wall covering front and back. The washer and dryer are hidden behind cabinet doors, side by side beneath a deep counter that holds a portable television. Overhead, track lighting is angled over the work areas.

The kitchen's library of cookbooks stand neatly shelved on the wall beside the window. Storage has been carefully thought out to save the cook's time and energy. Dishes and flatware are stored steps away from the dishwasher. Not shown is a wall-hung cabinet that stores crystal, trivets, and demitasse cups close to the dining table, and a floor-to-ceiling pantry that's two cans deep.

Photo: Norman Nishimura/Design: Fred Feinstein & Elaine A. Flug

The refrigerator, double oven, and pantry
with elegant small-paned doors are placed together to reduce step-taking. The sink is placed
so that the cook can overlook and chat with the
family or guests. Decorative ceramic tiles with a
bird motif are used to cover the counter tops.
The wet bar also serves as the children's sink,
keeping kids who cook out from underfoot. In
the dining area, two greenhouse windows display ferns, herbs, scented geraniums, and succu-
lents. The greenery is a cool and lovely background for the blond oak dining table set with
stoneware from Finland. The ceiling fan not only
adds to the old-fashioned look of the room, but
also keeps the room cool all summer. The half-
curtain at the back door was pieced together
from crocheted doilies.

▼ In this updated 90-year-old kitchen, a marble-like covering was used for the counters. A small-print wallpaper, matching window blinds, and painted strip on the cabinets enhance the old-fashioned look of the kitchen. But new appliances and track lighting increase its efficiency. Framed product labels hang on the wall above the appliances.

Photos: Carl K. Shuman/Design: Thomas Hills Cook

Before being remodeled, this kitchen had cracked walls, stained counter tops, and a worn floor covering. Even worse, the inefficient old kitchen had almost no counter surfaces. To remedy these problems, the room was covered with ceramic tile. Above and beyond its handsome appearance, ceramic tile is a remarkably practical material for a kitchen. It's fireproof—impervious to damage from heat even if you set a straight-from-the-oven pot on it. It doesn't stain and most kinds won't ever scratch, which eliminates the need for cutting boards. And for clean up, a few swipes with a damp sponge takes care of spills and crumbs.

Two ceramic tiles are used in this kitchen: rich brown glazed tile with a handcrafted look for the floor and built-in counter; solid glazed tile combined with a coordinated decorated tile on the old counter. Cabinet doors and the adjacent wall are covered with blue denim vinyl wallpaper and are further enlivened with art prints covered with protective clear plastic. Once stark white, the refrigerator was spray-painted to make it blend into the background. To give the small kitchen a more spacious appearance, small, cut-to-measure panels of lightweight mirror are mounted on the wall to the left of the refrigerator, visually "doubling" the room's tiny size.

t's hard to believe that this beautiful kitchen in a renovated townhouse was once a disaster, with peeling linoleum, old appliances, chipped porcelain, a door that didn't close properly, and a small leaky bathroom. The original bathroom was taken out, leaving a large open space with plenty of light for the cooking area. The kitchen cabinets are six inches higher than usual to suit a tall family. A wooden enclosure to match the cabinets is built around the trash compactor. An unusual feature of this kitchen is the "pet center," which has two bins: one for pet food, the other for kitty litter. Each bin has a chute that is opened by pulling a catch, allowing food to fall into the tray and the kitty litter to fall into a pan. The refrigerator is placed next to the dishwasher, so that all the appliances are within working distance of one another. A butcher-block table was cut to size, tied to legs made from plumbing pipe painted flat black, and placed in the center of the working area. A combination light and pot rack—incorporating plastic plumbing pipe, steel chain, and two rectangular wrought-iron pot racks with hooks—fits over the butcher block. This allows pots, pans, woks, and other kitchen accessories to be within reach of the sink or stove.

Radiators are enclosed in wooden boxes, and two benches and a table are used for meals. The benches are built to fit precisely into the corner. To insure easy entrance and exit to and from the seats, the table legs are mounted on casters and the table is attached with two springs to the radiator. The table can thus swing ten inches to the left or the right while remaining stable.

Photos: Robert C. Lautman/Design: Richard E. & Lorena Heizmann

▲➤ The old ceiling was pulled down and the original joists removed. To add color and to break up the otherwise sterile area, false beams were constructed by splitting the original joists, staining them, and screwing them directly into the ceiling with long toggle bolts. The holes for the bolts were then doweled, and the beams ended up looking as though they support the ceiling.

Pattern plays a major role in livening up this small, old kitchen. Every surface—cabinets, tile counters, and floor—is handpainted. A wine, rust and·lime star flower stencil design is applied to the white cabinets. The counter is painted rust with white star flowers to underscore the effect. The old linoleum is covered with a base coat of rust latex deck paint; wine, rust, white, and lime floral and linear designs are superimposed in washable acrylic with a top coat of polyurthane to seal the finish. Reiterating the theme is the co-ordinating stencil pattern that is painted on the ice cream table, chairs, and curtains.

A sloping ceiling of rough-sawn cedar siding in the breakfast room is in handsome harmony with the red-painted kitchen ceiling, which is textured with ready-mix joint compound. A row of windows brings a spectacular view to the table. Designs of oversized fruits are cut from the same fabric as the Roman shades, then glued to plywood. The kitchen combines old-fashioned touches—like the ceiling fan/light combination—with 20th-century conveniences, including the polyurethane-finished parquet floor, no-frost refrigerator, continuous-cleaning oven, and battery-operated wall clock.

Photos: Alan Hicks

T ake a tired-looking old kitchen, add crisp white walls, greenery, and a bright counter, and you've got a new room without the expense of tearing out walls or buying a roomful of new appliances. If your kitchen works well, as far as layout of space and circulation go, but lacks vitality, this is the route to take. Use paint, floor covering, new counters, and decorative accessories. Keep it uncluttered, and hunt for the pleasurable instead of the merely utilitarian.

Photos: Harold Kilgore/Design: Janet Cork

In this kitchen, an inexpensive counter top in terra cotta shade sets the tone for the color scheme. The glass-topped table with bamboo-shaped legs adds a garden touch and is light enough not to overwhelm the room, which is less than nine feet wide. The storage and work space are concentrated along one 15 1/2-foot wall. The room's light walls maximize sunlight, which is controlled by bamboo blinds. The dark floor of simulated brick and the ruddy counter anchor the room and give it an earthy look. Greenery and fresh vegetables, as well as jars of pasta, are used ornamentally. A yellow étagère displays plants and keeps cookbooks close at hand.

Crisp white blinds lend a contemporary air to this rustic kitchen and are easy to clean. An added advantage is that, when opened, they virtually disappear to admit the maximum amount of light and air. The kitchen work space is tucked in a corner of this kitchen/dining area. The U-shaped arrangement allows all appliances to be within easy reach. The long counter is useful as a serving space, and as an area in which the cook can work while still talking to company and family members.

Many old houses have oddly shaped windows that are a challenge to cover. Here, vertical bamboo blinds are used over a tall, skinny kitchen window.

Photo: Vince Lisanti

71

A background of white with bold splashes of strawberry and spring green bring excitement to this dining nook nestled in the corner of a kitchen. The fruit theme is enhanced by the fake fruit in the bowl on the shelf and in the basket by the ironing board. Gardening reminders are everywhere—in the plant pictures on the walls, the greenery placed strategically throughout the room, and the watering can on the shelf.

This old-fashioned kitchen is in a renovated loft apartment. A peeling plaster wall was removed to expose the original brick; green linoleum flooring was lifted to uncover the original wood floor; and acoustical ceiling tile was found to be covering up a turn-of-the-century pressed tin ceiling. A 19th-century pie-cooling cabinet is used in the kitchen to store china. The regulator clock and kitchen ceiling lights are castoffs of the New York public schools. The dining area has an oak table and chairs and a Tiffany-style lamp.

Photo: Everette/Design: Ellen Frankel & J. Christopher Jones

Chapter 5
Kitchens in Small Spaces

Those blessed with a large kitchen have no trouble finding room for storage, appliances, breakfast table and chairs, and lots of counter space. But a small kitchen is less flexible and has to be carefully designed to be as efficient as possible without making the cook feel too cramped.

Design: Eleanor Dunlop

This kitchen is small but not closed in; it can be seen from just about every point on the first floor of the house. The cabinets and grassy green counter tops coordinate with the colors used throughout the house. Combined with the slick black oven door and ventilation hood, they "dress up" this open area. The vegetables on the wall covering add a little old-fashioned kitchen charm.

A built-in, half-moon bar, with an easy-care plastic-laminate top, is a convenient place for breakfast or snacks. The attractive dining chairs have bronze velvety nylon seats. Their wicker backs coordinate with the wicker trays and baskets on the counters throughout the kitchen area.

Photo: Darwin K. Davidson/Design: Patricia Hart McMillan

In this kitchen, a subtle wall covering in beige and soft orange lends a small geometric pattern to the room. The small space is made efficient by the use of a counter-top microwave oven, a 30-inch drop-in range with self-cleaning oven, and a large capacity/built-in dishwasher. The choice of light oak rather than dark oak cabinets also helps enlarge the small area. Corner cabinets open to reveal rotating shelves, which increase usable storage space. Lights under the glass-fronted cabinets over the sink and in the slant-top stove ventilation hood properly illuminate the stove and sink work areas. The hood slips back to the vertical position when not in use, which automatically causes the fan and light to go off. The kitchen is open to the living room via a pass-through counter, which is sheathed in sleek orange plastic laminate.

A washing machine and dryer are conveniently located near all the other appliances in this kitchen, but are hidden from view in an extra-deep closet. The closet doors are covered in the same plaid paper as the kitchen walls; when the closet is closed, the doors are barely noticeable. The same wall covering is used inside the laundry nook as well.

Photo: Darwin Davidson/Design: Barbara K. Thorsen

Stools are kept handy for kitchen kibitzers in this kitchen so that the cook won't feel isolated. Although the kitchen working area is not large, the U-shaped area has been designed for convenience. And the high ceiling and large windows keep the area light and airy looking. A collection of graphics and an 1812 wooden works clock decorate the kitchen. To give a "furniture" look to the Formica-clad cabinets, the counter tops are the same color as the cabinets. Below the cabinets, drawers in varying sizes stash all the kitchen equipment. A cooktop is built into the island so that the cook can converse as he or she works. Track lighting and fluorescents under the cabinets can be dimmed at dinner parties. Next to the clock is a pull-out Parson's table that is handy for extra work space or as a serving table.

Photos: Vince Lisanti/Design: Nance Randol Interiors

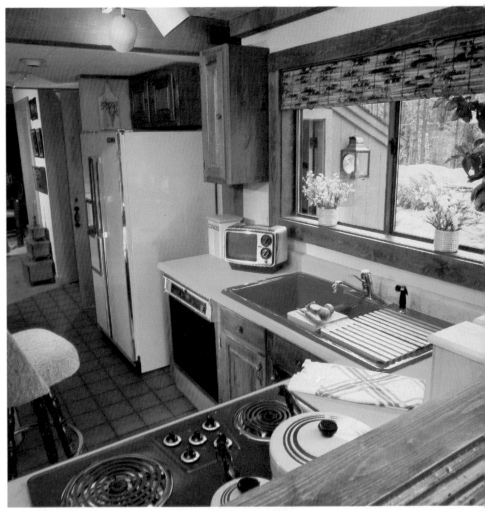

ere's a kitchen in a renovated barn with a wonderful view of the surrounding woods. Country rustic cabinets with gleaming brass hardware blend beautifully with sleek modern appliances. The warm redwood color of the sink is echoed in the no-wax vinyl flooring and in the slate-faced telephone, which has a place to hold the telephone book. Sleek counter tops of light avocado plastic laminate and the black glass fronts of the oven and dishwasher contrast with the texture of the bamboo blinds and wood accessories. The space-saving cooktop has five heating elements, one extra for a tiny saucepan. For breakfast or snacks, a bar stool upholstered in nubby, stain-repellant fabric conveniently swivels up to a counter built for two.

Photos: Everette Short/Design: John Mascheroni & J. Christopher Jones

This small kitchen has been turned into a childlike, fun place to be with the use of paint-box colors—orange, yellow, and green. The sculpture-look table and chairs, and the paper maché sculpture add to the room's fun.

Generally, light colors are recommended to visually expand small spaces. However, in this kitchen brown is the dominant color. There is brown wallpaper with a stylized white flower motif. Dark-stained, custom-designed cabinets contrast smartly with the ceramic tile floor. Brightly colored cookware and canisters adorn the easy-care counter top. Brown window blinds give the effect of color continuity across the windows. A tall stool pulls up to the short counter for a snack or coffee break.

Photos: Darwin Davidson/Design: Evan Frances, ASID, & Sally Alcorn

Photos: Ernest Silva Studio/Design: Jerry Hanover & Joseph Minicucci

Chapter 6
Utility Rooms and Storage Ideas

Having nearby space for a laundry room, sewing and craft center, large pantry, or additional storage closets turns an ordinary kitchen into a luxury one. With some ingenuity, closets can be converted into nooks for washing machines and dryers; steel shelves can turn ordinary closets into pantries; and work and craft areas can be set up alongside of kitchen appliances.

This red and orange tiled kitchen was designed with a craftsperson in mind. It features a craft corner, with a work table covered in ceramic tiles and surrounded by all necessary supplies. Wire baskets and white stack drawers hold materials, supplies, and tools. And there are plenty of shelves to store instruction books. The kitchen is a logical place for a crafts area because spills can be easily cleaned without worry of stains on the floors and tables. The ceramic floor tiles are set in a herringbone style for a dramatic pattern underfoot. The crafts corner is conveniently located for other functions as well—for use as a planning desk, mending center, or telephone table.

This "no-color" kitchen has white tile flooring, white louvered shutters, white cabinets, and white table and chairs. On the counter top, a white enamel juicer and glass and clear Plexiglas accessories melt quietly into the white background. The one-color scheme permits the eye to sweep, uninterrupted, around the room. The room seems larger; the walls appear to recede, the space to expand.

In addition to expanding the look of space in the room, the one-color scheme intensifies the color accents—the yellow chair seats seem more yellow, the long vertical bands of tape punctuating the shutters seem more green.

Keeping an all-white kitchen floor like this one clean was once a huge task. But now there's an all-white material that makes white flooring more practical—a vinyl asbestos with a permanent high gloss finish that needs no waxing. Just mop it lightly with a little soap or detergent, and it's clean.

The kitchen's center island is ingeniously created by a satellite counter that "floats" in mid-air—suspended from the ceiling by four shining polished steel rods. Although it looks as if it floats, the counter top itself is stationary and rigid enough for kitchen cutting, chopping, and slicing. No more hard-to-reach corners—this working space is approachable from all four sides, creating a space that's just right for salad-making, batter-mixing, and sit-down snacking.

Another thing there's less of in this kitchen is furniture legs. Only one tall stool has the conventional four-legged look. It is a convenient perch to pull up to the hanging counter for breakfast, and for times when the tired cook may want to make food preparations sitting down. The round pedestal table has no legs at all. And for seating, there are dining chairs that swoop down to semicircular bases. They provide all the comfort of the most classic over-stuffed armchairs, yet look light and airy. The round tabletop, the smaller round of the table base, and the unbroken curves of the armchairs echo the gentle semicircular arc of the shutter-covered wall behind

them. This makes a corner that's a pleasant medley of curves to soften the strongly angular lines of the flooring, the satellite counter top, and the built-in cabinets. The hanging cone-shaped light fixture poised over the table and the hanging baskets of greenery also provide a visual change of pace from the strong vertical lines of the steel rods that support the counter top and the floor-to-ceiling strips of tape that divide the louvered shutters. There's eye interest, too, in the long beams evenly spaced across the ceiling. A second set of ceiling beams dropped over the dining area serves subtly to divide the area into two parts: one for work, and one for eating.

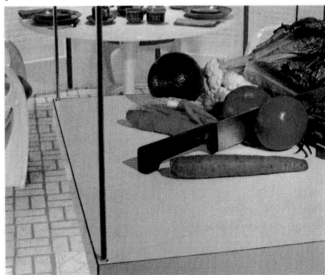

Photos & Design: Everette Short

Handy, ventilated, vinyl-coated steel shelves, an energy-efficient fluorescent light fixture, and louvered doors turn a closet in the laundry into this sewing center. The shelves hold rush boxes and canisters full of supplies. The closet also stores muddy boots and sloppy coats. The yellow-gold paint brightens the windowless area. Through the door, you can glimpse the kitchen. The vinyl asbestos flooring that covers kitchen, laundry, and sewing room is hardy and easy to clean.

Photo: Everette Short/Design: Evan Frances, ASID, & J. Christopher Jones

Photo: Everette Short/Design: Ellen Frankel & J. Christopher Jones

Smooth cedar walls and slate textured flooring combine with the floral wall covering to impart a light, bright outdoors feeling to this utilitarian space. More than a laundry room, it serves as a horticultural center and a "mud" room, with access through the garage or kitchen. Vinyl-coated steel shelves hold gardening equipment as well as laundry equipment. Sunny yellow blinds cover the door, and track lights are aimed at the appliance area.

Photo: Floyd Jillson/Design: June Gussin

Here's a closet every cook would love to have near the kitchen. It's conveniently set up to hold pots, pans, serving pieces, all small electrical appliances, and paper goods. The shelves are easy to clean and well ventilated. A vacuum cleaner fits neatly on the floor below the bottom shelf.

This laundry area has no-wax vinyl flooring with a textured finish that takes heavy traffic and hides scuff and heel marks. Cabinets hold laundry supplies, an ironing board, and extra linens.

Existing end walls of the garage and kitchen became the walls of this breezeway workspace. Two new walls, a roof, and a ceramic tile floor were all that were needed to create this handy room. It has a small desk area and plenty of storage space for plants and gardening equipment.

Photos: Vince Lisanti/Design: Nance Randol & Joanne Kinn

The door next to the hanging magazine rack in the dining area leads to a laundry room, which has a coffee-colored washer and dryer. The acoustical ceiling tile has a beige-on-white textured pattern. The wallpaper in the laundry room coordinates with the floral curtains in the breakfast nook. Towels restate the color scheme and the floral motif, and the fire extinguisher adds another dash of yellow. For extra convenience, there's a sink in the yellow cabinet behind the laundry room door.

Photo: Floyd Jillson/Design: June Gussin

A storage room off the kitchen has been turned into this laundry and sewing area. White paneling transforms the room into a light, pleasant working area. A sewing table in an L shape accommodates a portable electric typewriter as well as a sewing machine. Vinyl-coated, steel-ventilated shelving gives protection from mildew, dust, insects, and stale air.

A corner of this large kitchen has been turned into a work and storage area. Track lights illuminate the room.
Photo: Randolph Graff/Design: Elizabeth Matthews

Blue and white china and patchwork patterns are pulled together by the use of a small-scale, blue-on-beige print wall covering. A bureau is used to store place mats, napkins, and other accessories. Shelves above the bureau hold canisters of sugar and flour. A chair with table arm is a perfect place for the cook to rest and have a cup of coffee.

Photo: Keith Morton/Design: Scruggs-Meyers & Assoc.